Marie, The Bright Queen

Claudia Smith
Illustrated by Denise Muzzio

Marie, the Bright Queen

Copyright © 2019 Queen Girls Publications, LLC

Library of Congress Control #: 2018937773
ISBN: 978-0-9985047-8-0

Written by Claudia Smith | Illustrations and Design by Denise Muzzio | Edited by Victoria O'Malley

All rights reserved. No part of this book may be reproduced in any form or by any means, electronic or mechanical, including photocopying, recording, or by any information storage and retrieval system, without permission in writing from the publisher.

Printed and bound in Taiwan.

For bulk discount inquiries, please contact sales@queengirlspublications.com.

www.queengirlspublications.com

TO ALL THE GIRLS AROUND THE WORLD,

BE BRAVE
AND
SHINE BRIGHT!

Long ago, in a faraway land, lived a curious and intelligent girl named Marie. Her mom taught her to love books, but it was her dad that introduced Marie to her biggest passion... physics! Physics opened up a world full of experiments and incredible discoveries!

Every day after school, Marie headed straight to her dad's lab to see the MAGICAL experiments he was working on.

"When I grow up I want to be a physicist just like you dad!"

It was here, in her dad's lab, where Marie met Lulú.

Marie really wanted to study at a university, but it wasn't going to be easy for her. The university that admitted girls was far from home, and her family couldn't afford to send her there.

After much consideration, Marie had an IDEA. She spoke with her older sibling, Brosnia, and they agreed to help each other out.

They would take turns working a job in order to pay the other's tuition.
The deal was ON!

Brosnia was the first to study, so Marie began to work as a teacher. During these years, she worked hard and was able to pass on her passion for science to her students.

As it turned out, Marie enjoyed teaching very much.

But whenever she had a chance, she would run to the lab to conduct experiments!

Some years later, after Brosnia graduated, Marie's turn to attend university finally arrived.

It was her moment to begin the biggest adventure of her life: studying physics in college!

Marie was very excited, but a bit nervous as well. She had never been so far away from home...

Marie's fears disappeared the very moment she arrived at university. She knew she belonged there!

Marie's dedication paid off and she finished her studies in only three years! She was so bright that she didn't take long to get her first job researching whatever she wanted.
She felt on top of the world!

Marie decided to study the mysterious rays that came out of a recently discovered rock that radiated heat and light. Marie called this phenomenon radioactivity.

While doing this, Marie discovered two other rocks that turned out to be even stronger. Marie realized that the shiny rays might be used in medicine...

"Are you suggesting that they be used to treat ilnesses?"

Indeed, these rays could be used to cure many illnesses!
Her peers looked at her with astonishment. Never before had a woman achieved such an accomplishment!

The entire world was grateful, and from then on, Marie was known as THE BRIGHT QUEEN!

MARIE CURIE
Lived from November 7, 1867 to July 4, 1934.

She was the first woman to receive two Nobel prizes for her discoveries. She was also the first woman professor at a university.